Those People

Those People

Jenn Marie Nunes

DHP
Oregon

TNPRP
an imprint of DHP
Post Office Box 670, Warrenton, OR 97146

Those People
Copyright © 2020 Jenn Marie Nunes

All rights reserved

No part of this book may be reprinted without the express written permission of the publisher.
For permissions, contact DHP, Post Office Box 670, Warrenton, Oregon, 97146.
Printed in the United States of America

ISBN 978-1-935716-47-1

Cover art under license from Valentina Photos / Shutterstock.

CONTENTS

FAQ 9
Q: Why did you come here? 11
Q: Did your house flood? 12
Q: Did your neighborhood flood? 13
Q: Where would you be without it? 14
Q: Who do the editors believe read their newspaper anyway? 15
Q: Why did you come here? 16
Q: Where would you be without it? 17
Q: Is that good or bad? 18
Q: Is it safe? 19
Q: Why did you come here? 20
Q: Why did they make Marie Laveau a hair dresser? 21
Q: Is it dangerous? 22
Q: Is that good or bad? 23
Q: Why didn't they come back? 24
Q: Do you feel safe? 25
Q: Where would you be without it? 26
Q: Where can I find a real local meal? 27
Q: Is that good or bad? 28
About 33

What if my own skin makes my skin crawl?
What if my own flesh is suburban sprawl?
- "Fiya" tUnE-yArDs

FAQ

Q: Why did you come here?
_____

A: It was a place you lived because you had ties there, because you were stuck there or because your job was. A communion hole uncovered in cartography. These who romantilize. Redecorate the stove top w/ glass carnations. Slucking gas from broken pipes.

                                                                                          It is our

party.

Q: Did your house flood?

A: We are ready to walk thru the sign storm arms open and arterials twined. We are not ready to admit the rabbits splitting marshmallow along the seams.

Grieving for the city of a city of a city of a city. Urban areas are meant to be spaces that are ever growing, changing and thriving. The only thing I see our unrealistic. Literally Rally's burgers whenever.

Riding bikes at all hours of the day, walking dogs, going to the music clubs and stores nearby. You stick your finger thru the tear in its skin. I used to do that because I had no car and I *had* to do that. Rite into walls.

Q: Did your neighborhood flood?

A: Now, my new white neighbors and other white people passing thru the neighborhood are outside all the time.

Exhibit: the court of three sistering. A time nick. Blick. McDizzle. Because of incidents like those, where I grew up wasn't some hip place you moved when you didn't know what to do with your life.   Or it's bone.

A veritable vessel. A vassal. Chance has no mammary. All Columbus and dick-strong. Those infertile Anglos. It wasn't a blank slate.

Q: Where would you be without it?

A: Oh, gosh. First, this piece is just poorly written. Basement rabbits go postal in the heat. Our grasp tightens. And it's not an oral history like the other. Well-recorded. Accounts of personal stories. According to   according to

Whose gone holler?

No 2 abjects can occupy the same place. Re-wrought-ing language. Unable to elegate French Fries. "Some stayed and some didn't."

Q: Who do the editors believe read their newspaper anyway?

A: You don't develop authentically American music, cuisine and culture by sanitizing the neighborhood. Sitting next to a young white male in a bar watching the ridiculous American Horror Story. Swooning café-au-lait and rum.

I've never felt so in myself and he turns to me and says I AM THE ONE THAT CONSUMES AND ELIMINATES

(will never watch again)

Q: Why did you come here?

A: I like Hunter rain boots. Also suck jewels down to a nub.

Master the flimsy herostache. Master the lessening of my experience, by way of this essay, because I'm not native. Coat my body in stain. My husband and I w/ money from our Northeast relatives. And other white people passing thru.

Something like mojitos. An "us-versus-them" mentality and citywide cliquishness. While I used to think Halloween was the only holiday to require a mask.

Q: Where would you be without it?
_____

A: We come up in the year of loose horizons. Purporting the culture of violent nostalgia as the "real" is terribly dangerous. Look out the window all you can see is mined.

"I'm not interested in anything they have to say because they have nothing to say except how to make the city better." Cascading yoga pants and neon sneakers. There were rabbits for basements. You know which one we followed.

Unable to light the drive-thru votive.

                                        Tomorrow inhabits the full Magellan.

Q: Is that good or bad?

A: Towerin' with bobbles and the clean white car. Pet the upholstery and quit referring to yourself as transplants. Quit tellin' us the dead.

I used to live in New York for 13 Years. We were doing what so many transplants are doing now. Perched on the café tablet. Snuggled in the hood light. What comes in presses out.

"Our cemeteries have become Disney land!" (Marie Laveau pink tomb!)

Droolz

Q: Is it safe?

A: Nowadays their incessant moralizing and self-righteousness. Now at days beneath the surfade is pure mass. A clutch of silver dolphins. A glo-stuck.

Centrifugally raced.

Now in daze expendages reassemble out of history. The problem with the most recent group of arrivals. I feel like they're trying to make their prescience known. A thousand hands ungodlike. The repent on your thumbs. Nowdays paddle straight. Ignore the sirens. Keep an eye on your gut.

Q: Why did you come here?

A: A GPS – that stands for global positioning system. We laugh about it every time.

Q: Why did they make Marie Laveau a hair dresser?

A: Either you love this city or you don't. There is no neutral ground.

We'll train 'em. Buy homes, raise a family, and help to build a solid middling class. An arm's length black race. Artfully draped pinned and tucked. A royal shopping experience. Without their (heaven forbid!) "innovative ideas."

Points to the shut-up button. Frame beveled by the wit of industry. And a little tip to the people posting defensive comments. For me it helped.

Q: Is it dangerous?
_____

A: "I still question my ability, my right, and my author(ity) to write about this town. Hooked is not the right word, and neither is trapped." Thanks also to:

"home is a complicated place."

Q: Is that good or bad?

A: If only they would leave their baggage benign.

Try tactile. Protusion of modern castle in the gut. Drenched in the fusillite. A halo of the changing vibe and complexion of my neighborhood. E-L-I-X-I-R. That was the name of granddaddy's shop.

"Vegan Gumbo? Noise Ordinance?

gTtfooh!"

Q: Why didn't they come back?

A: Poised on the rim of a jelly jar. Where'd your grandmother go to school? Your aunties? The worst of urban areas. It's all word-of-mouth. Lips marshmallowed over. Come on, editorial team. Stick your finger down our threat.

All the secrets are secrets. Then you get taxed out your family. A journey fêted. Each rabbit of lies. As if they are mutually exclusive.

I love this city.   Fold your hands and
let's prey.

Q: Do you feel safe?

A: I feel like they are trying to make their presence known. Still warm in the cup of your palm. Tourism is all this city has.

Tucked into pearls. Rub one out in solidarity. There are ways to ride safely in the city.   Ingroups. How illuminous. How woh.

Q: Where would you be without it?

A: Agog. And several other names you can't remember.   But I do. I remember.

Q: Where can I find a real local meal?
_____

A: It's time to stop pitting "culture" against "progress." We're looking for a community. Still warm bodies. The vitality, the vibrancy,

                                                     the very sold.

There has always been this port city, nationality-switching, kind of chimeric, weird element.   "I can't even pronounce"

I have mixed feelings. "I would like to eat Eggs Benedict on a stick." It's terribly sad.

Q: Is that good or bad?

A: The renaissance is shifting away. Mall after mall after mall after maul.

Cradle its limp burst body under your shirt. People in the East have to eat, too. With the Walmart coming, and the hospital coming and there being schools out here. Who knows what'll schtick.

Why are the shutters always closed. And music does change. Lick its lids or knock louder. Suck the sweet phlegm from its nostrils. And knock louder. It is such a beautiful place.

[WHEN LOVE FOR A PLACE IS NOT ENOUGH]

[WHEN GOOD INTENTIONS ARE NOT ENOUGH]

[WHEN THE MASK OF KNOWLEDGE IS NOT ENOUGH]

[WHEN THE MASK OF IGNORANCE IS NOT ENOUGH]

[WHEN NEITHER MONEY NOR YOUR LACK OF MONEY IS ENOUGH]

[WHEN KNOWING THOSE PEOPLE IS NOT ENOUGH]

[WHEN STEPPING OUT IN SOME CONFUSED JOY IS NOT ENOUGH]

[WHEN SAYING HULLO LIKE YOU SEE EACH OTHER ON THE STREET IS NOT ENOUGH]

[WHEN WALKING ALONE THROUGH THE HOT NIGHT IN YOUR SO OPEN BODY IS NOT ENOUGH]

[WHEN PRONUNCIATION IS NOT ENOUGH]

[WHEN YOU WALK OUTSIDE AND SEE NOTHING IS NOT ENOUGH]

[WHEN KNOWING OF VIOLENCE IS NOT ENOUGH]

[WHEN KNOWING VIOLENCE IS NOT ENOUGH]

[WHEN BEING TOLD OVER AND OVER IS NOT ENOUGH]

[WHEN LISTENING QUIETLY IS NOT ENOUGH]

[WHEN TRYING IS DEFINITELY NOT ENOUGH]

[WHEN PUTTING THE LANGUAGE IN YOUR MOUTH IS NOT ENOUGH]

[WHEN PUTTING THE LANGUAGE IN YOUR MOUTH IS TOO MUCH]

[WHEN THE FILM OF YOUR SKIN IS TOO MUCH]

[WHEN YOUR DESIRE IS TOO MUCH]

[WHEN MY FAILURE IS WAY TOO MUCH]

ABOUT

we came before the birds came
back. everywhere
the ground was soft and wet w/
poison. everywhere
else the wonder slung waist high. it
was sick too
but we didn't care. we found a
thousand toothbrushes
and filled an empty cooler w/ red
lipstick fake
eyelashes and gin. we dragged it
home
and got drunk in our fancy
underwears w/ our
new face. we fell in love w/
ourselves.
everything else
was dead. then i knew i was. it was
time to celebrate

first   i   had   a   body flaccid

under the wet leaves.   i had a construction site and a café

full of big blowsy men ready handling.   we had a body we could settle

new   face   sexy   bonbon   lid-torn

the eye-sockets fringed in gold and blue X X   unaligned   w/ architecture.

we could walk thru our walls and feel

nothing. you could not.   dear it was velvet quiet at night so who ate off your heels. the lights gone up on my portmanteau. rabbits poured out from under the houses.   we just   want   to   fit our half

in yours and   baby
        SHUN

now it's all full of glitter
      UN-SHUN!   like
shrapnel.   I'm listening
that first bird call

when i say you i mean everyone.
when i say you
i mean lover. when i say you i mean
owner. when i say you i mean other.
when i say
you i mean those who stayed.
dear   those who stayed. carved
out and ready planning.   when
i say you i mean those who came
back.   the white page
yaws i say you
i mean anger.   beyond   our
walls it is
crawling. the city is beautiful if
you've gathered
all white.
                    it's beautiful to
me.
still
and claim it.   our   body
willing. bowed
open.   a   violin   gist   pockets
overflowing
w/ caul. join you for daiquiris and

Peruvian lime. our body
    riddled
luxurious the rotten beams
sprouting a timetable of salvageable
mercies
  but me   me

i swear

i'm like you.   but i've torn every page from the book of families made a nest of lay down by the toilet my head under the sink.

how sick   do you have to be as if generations never seen a plane up   close   flightless cobbled up a ringing   in our blood

we tapped the line we wiped the leaves from our pallid face w/ a piece of glass   and stuffed our fingers   down our throat

now the carousel of capital

                              turning

into   the

afternoon sun

there   is   only   this   moment fat as   celebrity   i swear i'm like you.

i ride the wolf in and lay down by the toilet

my head under   my head under the sink.
to ride this ride you must
       carry
              some risk

RE:

I CANNOT $$ MY CHILDREN
TO THE SCHOOL. I CANNOT MY
BROKE ASS. THOSE PEOPLE

so who snuck back first to assess
you   righteous.   on   the   balcony
overlooking
the dead refrigerators who smoked
a cigarette
who anointed the joints w/ glue. this
is where
we're born again. the chaffing meat
turned over in the static
sky   the
sinkhole
a-rattle w/ empty shells. the would
rarefied in wound

engulfed in whether i ventriloquate.

how does it feel to hear the story reflected?   a quick scan of people commenting on this post and they're people

who moved here from somewhere else just not so recently.   not to gloat but

my family is full of real-estate. i feel bad for the poor

      i do.   who carries cash   now in days   we'd rather slick

the mask w/ stolen cover-up release lanterns riding fire into the night

                                          sky.
i mean the streets get paved nowdays i mean

i stole what's mine the city's

mine. i've sauntered thru the killing pool. the braille of

guns   parse   my   air

that stuff on the balcony? it's all lies.

i took

the memories and plastic floaties and

built

you a grown-ass prom and still a

reason to get

angry.

green water and the halls split

simple

soon comes the chorus.

soon

comes the chorus the terrible

chorus soon   the only thing you

want

to die.

better gather jade for luck. you're the

one

told   me   to   fuck   off

RE:

I CANNOT AFTER SIX YEARS
EXPERIENCE. I CANNOT IN MY OWN
PALAZZETTO. THOSE PEOPLE

grammar is political. i can hear
your difference.   subtle hunger
built an inland sea the subjectivity
of   *gurrrl*. built
before test tubes from the bones
of animals you didn't know were
animals
        pale like that fresh coat
all primed and i'm not thankful what
was coaxed from grown men
gurrrl
        what ward we wrung
rooftop to dirge. anxious
        the dog
stench has layers. those puppies
been split open like packaging.
beneath my spare
ribs a safe of dead buttons. *gurrrl*.
        my mashed
potato mouth been run on.
this glitter
don't never   come   out

let me articulate   elbow elbow
wrist wrist   elbow
elbow wrist
wrist the author of
Walmart's not
subtle. our body goes under
comes up w/ your rite.
it's tedious
but we don't hate you for trying.
                        we don't
have to.
we slide between slats and we're prolly
immortal. alarm chimes out our cavity
sweetly and dull. down south the wolf doubles. broken mirrors line our spine.   you can't fight big boxes can't not super size
                thus
we paint our face
w/ plunder. they say you are what you   eat.
i believe
this place will eat me.

            you can believe whatever you want

RE:

I CANNOT MAKE THE WEEDS
EDIBLE. ABIDE SNOBBERY. THOSE
PEOPLE CANNOT STAND OUT

on the wharf　　　　dear chorus
　　　　　　no one knows me
dead dogs is periphery the carpets
licked clean. our ring finger's worn
down
to the bone.　　　the truth is
dear chorus
　　　　　　　i came after
　　　　my memories are boxes
i stole from Walgreens. it starts
soaked in water then
the wolf marked our wrist.
　　　　　　　　　dear chorus
　　　　　　i want to stay here
time to peel out the skin.
don't worry　　　we're happy
to spray tan our pestilence eat out the
fastener
and slip thru your window to sleep

we're so

fêted

pride-fat at high tide. Walgreens
ain't shucked. we can't test our
pregnancy over
or under w/o being unlocked.
 to keep
their prices low. suspended from
your own
 for days. full up w/ jazz
hands. please believe
i know
nothing. the wolf mouths
our ankle its teeth find no
tune. arise and go streaming from
plastic applicator stick
down to moon. for realz.
drink light from the mirror. i love
but i don't know
nuthin
from books from magazines who
knelt
your vitriolic crinoline your plastic
go-
face. hand me a cup

to-go

to-go

to-go

RE:

THOSE COPY CANNOT GRIEF.
CANNOT W/ A GUITAR
OR DREAM. WTF EULOGY

everyone who writes about this

place is a liar. so am i. a storm made us

reverb. but it was human. now the voices extend

our outsider. someone has to fill what

the birds left. i shit in all the rooms.

                                      dear chorus

now the edges brim
w/ white
noise

RE:

I CAN'T NOT BLACK
PEOPLE. CULTURE. I CANNOT
W/ MY OWN FACE

RE:

I CANNOT ARTISANAL DAIQUIRIES. I
CANNOT 2-FOR-1 ANYTHING. RE
SETTLE. RE PURPOSE

go on

click the link.

even the birds are angry but that's what you want.

a swatch of puritan			credit.

you're here and you're here and here beneath the dome bone

		salting your beans

and your gin. let's make out w/ lead window dressings. make

a   suitcase   full   of   everyday   pap. proud

knight. the song sweet moon

sickle   like   how   humans   tooled   up. the moon scythe

dear Walmart neighborhood. dear planning committee i'm not leaving this time.

i'll never leave you

again

so open our mouth

and click singing. sometimes   our voice is on fire. a clean

blue   flame. i   won't   claim   our body.   ashamed   of   what's   been consumed.

fever   meat.   family   homes.   i've watched

them build buildings w/ their own hands. that's not

what   makes   you   belong.
          but don't listen to me.

the   projector's   misfiring.   we   click singing. full up w/ contagion. i'm just one sign

for a body   who cares

also the anarchists are crying
again.   dear   chorus
that pumpkin is not yours unless you
grew up here
and/
or before bloody knuckles then hum
a secret tune   a $10
haircut   a shot
of Jim Beam   company handshake
an explosion of welcome mats
the   answer   is   never   *okay*.
time   to   light
the Pier 1 lights.
i am opening. barred but
for   your   offering.   thin   and
absorbent.
if we hold our breath the masks
the flags will start singing if we sing
sing   the Dollar Store martyr
will burst into flame. a warning
parade.   i'm   drunk   i'm
drunk on your dumb purchase

call the banner of sky purple

or blue. remember how we laughed at our

burned out parapet. tarred the

last muse.   there is no scene

but the scene circumscribed by punctuation.

time to agree on color. time to

get right w/   America why are you   so

racist?

god doesn't love you better than the fishes

RE:

PRIME ENTREPRENEURIAL.
ENECOSYSTEM. WILL NOT BUY
THOSE PRALINES
ON OUR BUS

RE:

THOSE PEOPLE CANNOT CALL
ONESELF. CANNOT GLAM CUSTOM.
THE SEVENTH WARD IS NEXT

o terror

watch instantly. nobody wants

to   be   handled   thru

high winds

rattle the banana fronds the wild

aisles at the Dollar General

are   more   real   than   god.

something i read recently.

rode the streetcar past the highway

and caught the body

public. a dog pressed out thru its own

holes. our body

getting high in the streetkid's turret

smoking e-cigarettes

to feel   alive. or it's done

married w/ crockpot finger bones

like cross-hairs

on a gun. sometimes you have to

say   it   and   say   it.

we were scared when the eyes silver

dollared.

here take this

shovel. put the possum out of its

misery.

what nature is on sale these days.

what

can you afford to feed your children

bold in the lines between those w/
a voice.   stripped of
insect   song
the sty ruh fohm cooler gets
a second coming. panty-hose to last a
generation. the Walmart
is always out of thread. we use it to
stich our tour
in palace. the cavernous Sunday
brunch filmed
by transplants and cast w/ regular
folk

us too

we're not a blank slate. the toothpaste castle

on my shoulder. the figurine shit in my sink. an alley of refrigerators yawning for

representation. here have some free lipstick here

have a drink. oops your human is showing. no one's crowning

to save you.

no one's click will refresh. the "refugees"

are glo-ing. hot to the touch. we'll patent

your failures your down time your blood.

make calls. induce calm. the ad venture. this stolen moon pie.

this stolen bloat. your dress a billowing speech.

 the severed head of a flower. legs dangle. we'll be both

under your skirts and on the roof shooting.

 Americans always assume guns

RE:

THOSE PEOPLE CANNOT LOVE
MY CITY. I CANNOT
METAPHOR

RE:

CERTAINLY NOT THE WHITE
PEOPLE. NOT MY WHITE
HUSBAND AND CAT

beneath the plastic

fragments of myth on display how

much $$ did we fist.   i

followed from stoop

to rumor   playground

       to the naked

water and my clothes unhinged.

       the door

collapsed and i grew me. green w/

enemy. me

and our body dividend. i didn't

want   over anything

only ruche a little along the edges.

elaborate

my   blank

meanwhile

our brunch has gone cold

now

                    now

now
                    totaled
on   throat   bones   and   the   stench
of lighting a match. outside
recedes   in   relief.   dear   integrity
shopping mall.
dear
shipping and loan. even w/o birds the
stars   are   meant
to be painful. and the city
is   meant   to   be   weak

RE:

I CANNOT WISH OUTSIDE
MY BODY. FUCK PIZZA.
THOSE PEOPLE

put that way everything around you
is art.

you grew up in romantic. you were
torn into body
glub
w/ absence run
the last blue ribbon
thru your hair. America's
not
not our America! we lit up its
unconscious. down there
or
the other down there.

i need to see it. i feel like i need
to see it

tiny fishes trim the dead skin
from your static. undulation. light throws
and the water-fat bodies of stuff
          show their tits. in the lake silence
gets braided. i got an oxygen mask for you
done up in pink puff paint. i've unmasked the spot
where mud slucks you down to the hips.   drink a beer in
this vintage petticoat. drink
a beer and get angry. kiss your murders good-
bye the bistros are coming   this tide fraught w/ pomme frites
w/ muggings
and Prius.
      at the pitch bottom
who's watching. the date-red light
frills to chill haze and every furniture
opens its legs. split like a bud
and frontal. you've lost your wane.
tiny fishes nibble right down
and refurbish. tiny fishes nibble right down to

RE:

I CANNOT GET KICKS W/O
GUNPOINT. I CANNOT LIVE
DOWN

RE:

THOSE PEOPLE CANNOT
BUILD IN OUR
I CANNOT NOT KIND RACIST

                              Shakespeare
taught me that love's   not about
gentrification. i didn't mean our
body   to condo in your
         bed. i didn't know
it   was   spreading.   but   look
pretty.
there's no trick here. we came from
elsewhere. moved into
your hood.   we said hood.
         it was funny
to me. then the sirens
got bolder.
i had some voice. neither did you.
the flesh chose me
like i asked to.   i write things
down cuz i have to.   who
made who
better.   more   historic

o terror

speak   out.

this is not how it is just because it is.

pluck   the   flowers

of   capital   from   the   slush

of your

skin.

pomegranates   halved   and

dripping

bones   as   hard   as   radio

silence no one is listening to the

plans   you   dream   smoking

cigarettes under the mothlight

w/   blood   on

all of our hands

stained now w/ enemy

o   terror   speak

straight from the glut

you were told a ceramics of

stars hung just out of reach   use

your   tools

human   tip   the   whole   constellation

from the sky

i say you should eat me.
i'm not sure it's the truth

i know you will eat me. i'm what's
not the truth

thought you'd ease on forever. i see
your   fingers   stretch

empty
your shame how misplaced

what's hard should be soft and
what's soft   should be

here   is the heron's leg.
          minus murder we're still

spangled w/ culture   the market
demand

a knife in your   back and the juice
is running down

you think that you see me you'd real
like   to   eat   me

&c. &c. &c.

RE:

I CANNOT SAUNTERING IN
NOT WHENEVER. NOT TO BRAG BUT
I'VE BEEN MUGGED TWICE AND
NEARLY MURDERED

RE:

I CANNOT AS SEEN IN THE NEW
FILM VERSION. WILDLIFE INVADES
POVERTY. I CANNOT "FRAND"

o

the tyranny of emergency she's sure
she's the sun. i saw her drink drain-
o
crack glass w/ her thighs. grown
cast iron titties
coins
on her tongue now she's put up in
storage
                nestled in neon watched till
she screens.   from
the queen
bed she pulls out a can-opener
a scrap of gutter   a son.
marble faced and soft-
bodied he goes on the mantel and
stinks
in the heat. everything stinks
in the heat. your neighborhood
smells like dog shit

you follow the umbilical cord glimmeringly

curious killed the.   the. sandwiched between our body in the

backseat of an old cop car. your baby's no

cop. first you had a story a rendezvous point on a map

then the sirens got bolder   we took the synapse the mouth feel

emergency   emergency

the jewelry behind her pulp. left her waxing

like a blow-up doll. she scents you spying

and gristles. can't see what this trade-in demands. deep cuts.

spun all night in your real human. your real human blah

      blahblahhh. our baby talk back baby she

emergency

she the reel. you try rewind try to project her. she just spins and spins

if you lost everything you might
double purchase. our body off
sticking fingers into its own
cut.   you watched and they
did.
who would take those humanity off
air. every front yard
                            fenced-off
not   every   step   outside
and the world is gone
plunge
your hands into
our body til it's up to your elbows
dear prophecy get buried. it's a two-
for-one   deal

RE:

I CANNOT KEEP HOLD OR
WORK LAWLESS. HE CANNOT SEE
AGAIN HIS COUSIN'S FACE

peat smolders in the east. i'll miss the scent.

our body coughs in your bed. roll over. face first

between McDonald's thighs. where the wealthy

built a cushion out of history and glass. our socks

are glass. or get right w/ restraint.

i can see our lipstick

wrought outside the line of bone but we feel

you've fallen for the vessel where sky meets. you have pounded an arc of delicacies. taste

of jewelry cooked in butter. put our hand inside. there was never any lock

never any key

RE:

THOSE PEOPLE THEY REAL LIKE
PICKLED
MEAT LIKE THEY REAL LOCAL THEY
GOT FUNERAL

o   terror
the children are listing
they know
how   to   light   their   voices
stay history
                  rebuild
a tear in trajectory a set of sky steps
past twinkling teacups a blackness
unveiled

what we want   now
is breath. the bellows

of   rib   cages.   our   body   rubs
bodies

w/ a handful of lard. fire take the
fever what   worked its way up

from your dressing gown. in what
would

                        let the ground give
way

for communion. i held her son
against the roof of my mouth.

how long does marble take to reach
body   temperature.   how   long

can the pelicans ride the highway
before they get flat.	surely you can

unburden. surely
the wet muscle of your mouth

will melt the vestibule as it works its
way		out of your throat

RE:

ENJOY YOUR STREETCAR TO NOWHERE
TOURISTS ENJOY OUR BEAUTY
SUPPLY YOUR ENJOY ENJOY YOUR ENJOY

ACKNOWLEDGEMENTS

Thank you to the journals in which versions of these poems first appeared:

NOÖ Journal: *from* About
Similar:Peaks:: *from* FAQ
Smoking Glue Gun: *from* About
Tupelo Quarterly: *from* About

Much of the language in "FAQ" is taken from interviews, articles, and the posted comments (many anonymous or posted under screen names) about New Orleans published online at *The Gambit*, *NolaStudiola* and *The Louisiana Justice Institute*, broadcasted on WWNO, and posted on Facebook. I have not always used quotes to indicate language that isn't "mine," but that does not mean I am claiming this language. The "I" of this book is neither my singular "I" nor is it some authoritative speaker who is speaking back to these "other" voices, trying to answer or correct. It is not that the book doesn't have a perspective, but that its perspective is various and flawed. I hope you will explore the original conversations I'm engaging.

You can find a list of links to articles and conversations, including but not limited to those mentioned above, about gentrification in New Orleans and gentrification more generally at the author's website: https://jennmarienunes.com/

This book represents years of living, thinking, and rethinking. And rethinking. I would like to thank some of the excellent humans who have supported this project in various ways, especially those that have pushed me to see the world differently and interrogate my place in it: Mel Coyle, Veronica Barnes, Anne Marie Rooney, Kristin Sanders, Meghan Ann McHugh, Maurice Ruffins, Laura Mullen, Norbet Davidson, Maria Romasco Moore, Lauren C. Robinson, Leah Robinson, and Terri Simon, whose willingness to take on consultation of this manuscript really made the book possible.

www.ingramcontent.com/pod-product-compliance
Lightning Source LLC
Chambersburg PA
CBHW050503110426
42742CB00018B/3351